THE OFFICIAL

®

England Rugby

ANNUAL 2019

D1338459

Written by Michael Rowe

Designed by Mathew Whittles

A Grange Publication

©2018. Published by Grange Communications Ltd., Edinburgh, under licence from the Rugby Football Union. The RFU Rose, the words 'England Rugby' and Ruckley name/image are official registered trade marks of the Rugby Football Union. Printed in the EU.

Photographs © RFU via Getty Images.

ISBN 978-1-912595-07-5

Contents

England Fixtures 2019

SIX NATIONS

Ireland v England
Saturday 2nd February,
Aviva Stadium, 16:45

England v France
Sunday 10th February,
Twickenham Stadium, 15:00

Wales v England
Saturday 23rd February,
Principality Stadium, 16:45

England v Italy
Saturday 9th March,
Twickenham Stadium, 16:45

England v Scotland
Saturday 16th March,
Twickenham Stadium, 17:00

RUGBY WORLD CUP

Japan, Pool C

England v Tonga
Sunday 22nd September,
Sapporo Dome

England v USA
Thursday 26th September,
Kobe Misaki Stadium

England v Argentina
Saturday 5th October,
Tokyo Stadium

England v France
Saturday 12th October,
International Stadium
Yokohama

Quarter Finals
Saturday 19th + Sunday 20th
October

Semi Finals
Saturday 26th + Sunday 27th
October

Final
Saturday 2nd November,
International Stadium
Yokohama

QUILTER SUMMER INTERNATIONALS

England v Wales
Sunday 11th August,
Twickenham

England v Ireland
Saturday 24th August,
Twickenham

England v Italy
Friday 6th September,
St James' Park

All times are UK times (GMT/BST)

WELCOME

to the Official England Rugby Annual 2019

2019 is a year full of promise for the England team.

There is no tournament like the Rugby World Cup. Japan 2019 will give us six weeks of incredible action and drama. Maybe, just maybe, England will do what we all dream of and bring the trophy back to Twickenham.

2018 was a difficult year for the England team. After two years of almost unbroken success under Eddie Jones, the team had to dig deep to remain strong in the face of several defeats.

In rugby, adversity can change good teams into great ones. With England's depth of talent there is no doubt that they will emerge a stronger, more formidable team than ever before – worthy challengers for the RWC crown.

This book gives you the chance to look back on 2018 and look forward to 2019. It's packed full of profiles, pictures and activities to keep you informed and entertained.

If you love rugby you'll **really** love this annual.

Turn the page to start another great year of rugby action!

SIX NATIONS

ROUND 1

Venue: Stadio Olimpico
Date: 4th February
Result: Italy 15 / England 46

Seven tries gave England a solid victory in Rome, but a strong Italian performance meant the victory was not as comfortable as the scoreline might suggest.

Sam Simmonds scored two tries on his Six Nations debut, and Anthony Watson added a couple of his own. Owen Farrell, George Ford and Jack Nowell also scored.

The key sequence in the match came in the 51st minute. Italy had just crossed England's line, and could have moved to within three points of Eddie Jones' men, but the try was disallowed for a forward pass. Simmonds, who had been looking exceptionally sharp and eager all match, spotted a gap from a maul and used his devastating speed to secure England's fourth try and a bonus point.

Simmonds' try effectively sealed what had been a competitive match, and England piled on the points as the strength of their replacements began to tell and the Italians tired.

It was a pleasing start for an England team seeking a third successive Six Nations championship. The Ford/Farrell partnership looked rock solid - with both men turning in world-class performances. Jones will also have been pleased to see several players looking comfortable on their championship debuts. The only downside was a nasty knee injury to Ben Youngs.

Elsewhere, Wales gained a surprisingly easy win over Scotland. In Paris Jonny Sexton landed a 42 metre drop goal in the last minute to give Ireland a spectacular win over France.

REVIEW

ROUND 2

Venue: Twickenham Stadium
Date: 10th February
Result: England 12 / Wales 6

Jonny May scored his first-ever tries in the Six Nations to see England home in a tight match against a determined Welsh side.

Both of May's tries came in the first 20 minutes, and on both occasions he benefited from truly world-class build-up play. The first try came just two minutes into the match. A sublime cross-field kick from Owen Farrell left the Welsh defence helpless, and Jonny's speed and dexterity enabled him to collect the ball and cross the line in one fluid movement. The second score came as Joe Launchbury powered his way to the scoreline before popping a glorious pass to the unmarked May.

Having raced to a 12-0 lead, England then had to reach deep into the locker to contain a potent Welsh side. Wales were twice denied tries, once by a controversial TMO (Television Match Official) decision and once by a classic covering tackle from Sam Underhill. The end of the match came in an exhausting series of plays - with English tacklers repeatedly smashing the Welsh back behind the gain line.

The second round of the championship also saw victories for Scotland and Ireland, leaving the Irish top of the table on points difference.

ROUND 3

Venue: BT Murrayfield Stadium
Date: 24th February
Result: Scotland 25 / England 13

A day to forget for England.

In the 2017 match against Scotland England had been utterly dominant, winning every phase of the game with comfort and running out 61-21 victors. This year's match was very different, as England were comprehensively outplayed for the first time in Eddie Jones' reign.

Jones himself was frank after the game, giving credit to Scotland and admitting that the men in blue fully deserved their victory. England had no answer to the Scots' adventurous attacking play, conceding three tries in the first half. They were also outfought at the breakdown, particularly by the Scottish skipper John Barclay.

England came out strongly in the second half, with Owen Farrell crossing the Scottish line just three minutes after the break, but English indiscipline and committed Scottish defence meant Jones' men could not close the gap any further. The match was effectively finished when Sam Underhill was sinbinned for an illegal tackle and Finn Russell knocked over the resultant penalty.

England's defeat saw them lose ground at the top of the table to Ireland, who won at home to Wales. France beat Italy in Marseilles.

ROUND 4

Venue: Stade de France
Date: 10th March
Result: France 22 / England 16

Another defeat for England, but there was some comfort in a slightly improved performance from the men in white.

The game ended with Eddie Jones' men camped on the French line, desperately trying to score the converted try that would have given them a victory. Passionate French defence meant that England were kept at bay, and gave France a first championship win over Les Rosbifs in four years.

Jones had reacted to the Murrayfield defeat by making several changes to the side. Mike Brown was rested with Anthony Watson moving to full back and Ben Te'o came in for Jonathan Joseph in the centre. Skipper Dylan Hartley missed out through

injury – meaning that Jamie George made a well-deserved first start in the championship.

Both sides would end the match with 100% kicking records. The first half saw Owen Farrell and Elliot Daly on target for England, while Maxime Machenaud knocked three over for France. It was 9-9 at half time.

The game's decisive moment came in the second half, when France were awarded a penalty try following a high tackle from the yellow-carded Anthony Watson. Even with a late try for Jonny May England were never able to close the gap.

Ireland secured a bonus point victory over Scotland to secure the championship and Wales beat Italy.

ROUND 5

Venue: **Twickenham Stadium**
Date: **17th March**
Result: **England 15 / Ireland 24**

A disappointing performance from England allowed a clinical Ireland side to claim the Grand Slam. Snow was falling at Twickenham and the touchlines were painted blue in order to stand out clearly. Otherwise the stadium was pretty much green all over as Ireland secured their third-ever Grand Slam on a famous St Patrick's Day.

England could at least reflect on three tries, with two for Elliot Daly and one for Jonny May. Daly's first try came after a beautiful grubber kick from Owen Farrell and his second, after 64 minutes, gave England hope of securing an unlikely victory.

The three tries were England's only scores, with Farrell having something of an off-day from the kicking tee. Eddie Jones applauded the effort put in by his players - but was disappointed by the penalties given away at key moments and in key positions.

Jones was typically generous in his praise for the Irish side, conceding that they were the better team and had executed their game plan almost to perfection.

Wales just beat France to finish second and Scotland squeaked past Italy to claim third place. England had to be content with fifth, their lowest-ever Six Nations finish.

THE OFFICIAL England Rugby QUIZ!

England Rugby

HOW WELL DO YOU

Hint – all the answers are in this book, so why not come back when you have finished reading.

1 In which Six Nations game did Jonny May score his first tries?

2 In what year did England win the Rugby World Cup?

3 England are the only northern hemisphere side to have won the Rugby World Cup.

a) True ■   b) False ■

4 Where was the Rugby World Cup Sevens held in 2018?

a) Chicago ■
b) Las Vegas ■
c) San Francisco ■

5 What is England's highest ever score? (Tip, they played against Romania in 2001.)

KNOW YOUR RUGBY?

6 Which country is missing from the list of Six Nations competitors? England, Scotland, Wales, Ireland, France.

7 What trophy do England and Scotland play for?

a) Cook Cup ☐
b) Hillary Shield ☐
c) Calcutta Cup ☐

8 George Ford is the youngest ever player in a professional union game.

a) True ☐   b) False ☐

9 How many countries take part in the Rugby World Cup Sevens men's series?

10 In what year was the first Rugby World Cup held?

11 Who is England's most capped player?

a) Jason Leonard ☐
b) Rochelle 'Rocky' Clark ☐
c) Danny Care ☐

12 Who won the men's 2018 Six Nations?

a) Scotland ☐
b) Ireland ☐
c) Wales ☐

13 What is the capacity of Twickenham Stadium?

a) 65,000 ☐
b) 56,000 ☐
c) 82,500 ☐

14 What is the name of the 2019 Rugby World Cup Mascot?

15 How many points is a drop goal worth?

a) 5 ☐   b) 3 ☐   c) 6 ☐

Thanks to 10-year-old William Dixon-Minter for his help in testing the quiz.

HOW DID YOU DO?

Answers on page 60

13

JOE MARLER

Joe Marler is one of England's star props, with more than 50 caps.

Once famous for his colourful hairstyles, Marler is now regarded as one of the most powerful and experienced props in world rugby.

Marler normally plays at loose-head prop, wearing the No.1 jersey. Along with his tight-head prop and the hooker he makes up the front row - providing stability in the scrum and transmitting the force produced by his pack to the opposition forwards. The physical demands on a prop are immense, and front row players are often substituted to bring a fresh pair of legs (and lungs) into play.

Marler excels in the traditional skills of a prop - helping win ball at the scrum or lineout and knocking opposing players back over the gain line in defence. He knows that this is not enough, however, for the modern prop - who is also expected to offer a presence all over the field, comfortable in running and passing with the ball.

Since making his debut against South Africa in 2012, Marler has proved willing and able to change his game to become the type of player required by the England side. Even his once famous Mohawk hairstyle had to go when the England coaches pointed out it made it too easy for referees to spot him!

Competition for front row places, in the starting line-up or as a replacement, in the England team is fierce. Marler also knows that many of his rivals for the loose-head position, such as Saracens Mako Vunipola, are renowned for their dynamic contributions in the loose.

Such is the strength of Marler's contribution, however, that - injury and self-discipline permitting - he has every chance of turning out to help England in their 2019 Six Nations and RWC campaigns.

WORLD RUGBY

If you're going to Twickenham a trip to the World Rugby Museum is a must!

The museum tells the story of rugby from around the world, following the game's history from its origins to the present day. The new museum opened in February 2018 in the south stand at the world-famous stadium. It is bigger, better and more interactive than ever before.

One of the museum's highlights is the fantastic 'What Kind of Rugby Player Are You?' interactive zone.

Here you can test your kicking, speed, agility, power, strength and endurance. Find out if you are a powerful centre, a strong forward, a speedy winger or an agile full-back – there is a position for everyone!

The World Rugby Museum is the definitive home for everything and anything about rugby!

If you're visiting the museum on a non-match day you can combine your visit with a Twickenham Stadium Tour. A friendly, expert guide will show you all the best bits of this wonderful stadium, including the England dressing room and pitch side. Check availability before you visit.

Why not get your teacher to check out the museum's award-winning packages for schools and colleges – combine a visit to the museum, a stadium tour and a free, curriculum based workshop or seminar.

Make sure you visit worldrugbymuseum.com to find out more and get the latest information. Happy visiting!

The Six Nations can trace a lineage back to the very first **international** fixture between England and Scotland in 1871.

MUSEUM

CALCUTTA CUP

How to play

Test your kicking, speed, agility, power, strength and endurance

In the all-new World Rugby Museum you can:

- Explore a glittering array of **trophies** including the Calcutta Cup made from 270 silver rupees

- Take up the challenge of discovering "What Kind of Rugby Player are You?" in the **Play Rugby Zone**

- Re-live some of rugby's most **memorable moments** with film and video **footage**

- See the **oldest** international rugby jersey

- "Choose your own **World XV**" interactive

worldrugbymuseum.com

ANTHONY WATSON

Anthony Watson is a true speed merchant, whether playing on the wing or at full back. Few players can match his pace and he averages a try nearly every two games!

Anthony's route to the full international side included winning the IRB (World Rugby) Junior World Championship in 2013. Anthony was one of the stars of the England team, scoring a try to help beat New Zealand in the semi-final.

Stuart Lancaster, who was then England head coach, recognised Anthony's potential and invited him to join England's training squad for the 2014 Six Nations - when he was still aged only 19. Making his debut against New Zealand later that year, Anthony was soon established as England's first choice on the right wing.

Although most of his caps have come on the wing, he is equally at home playing at full back. He doesn't see a huge difference between the two positions - and his blistering pace, confidence under the high ball and positional awareness make him equally suited to either role.

2017 saw Anthony take on the ultimate challenge for any rugby player - a tour to New Zealand with the British and Irish Lions. The natural choice for the No. 14 shirt, he scored the Lions' first try of the tour and started all three tests. A thrilling series saw him enhance an already high reputation.

The Six Nations 2018 series was a major disappointment for England, and things couldn't have been much worse for Anthony, who suffered an Achilles injury which forced him to miss the tour to South Africa.

He is a multi-talented sportsman and athlete, who had trials for Chelsea FC. He is also a mad-keen NFL fan - and there have even been rumours of interest from major American Football franchises.

For the moment, though, everyone will need to look elsewhere. Anthony is 100% concentrated on winning RWC 2019 with England!

19

SEVENS

What a busy year for England's Sevens stars! England finished 8th in the HSBC Men's World Sevens Series and also competed at the Commonwealth Games and Rugby World Cup Sevens.

The HSBC Sevens is one of the most thrilling spectacles in world rugby. The men's series sees teams from 15 core countries compete in glamorous locations all around the world – including Hong Kong, Las Vegas, Dubai, Paris and London.

The action takes place on a full-sized rugby pitch. With only seven players on each side, there is plenty of space for the players to demonstrate their remarkable skill, athleticism and flair. Fans pack the stadiums to enjoy both the electrifying action and the party atmosphere.

The series came to a thrilling finale in Paris – the last event of the 2017/18 season. England had put in their best performance of the year, beating favourites Fiji in the quarter final and then overcoming Canada to secure a place in the final. Facing them were the South African Blitzboks – who needed a victory to win the overall title.

England took the lead in the first half, thanks to a brilliant try from Dan Norton, but South Africa struck back after half-time and managed to hold on to clinch a 24-14 victory and just pinch the series title from Fiji.

The action takes place on a full-sized rugby pitch. With only seven players on each side, there is plenty of space for the players to demonstrate their remarkable skill, athleticism and flair.

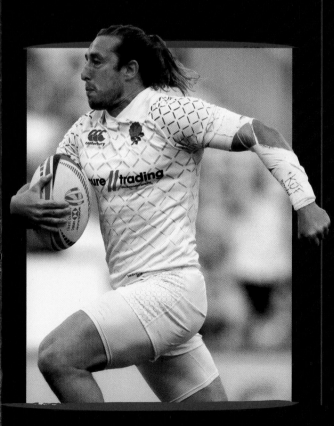

Women's Series

The 2017/18 women's series saw 11 core teams compete in 5 tournaments: Dubai, Sydney, Kitakushu (Japan), Langford (Canada) and Paris. England's women finished eighth – the same result as in the previous year. Australia clinched the series title, just pipping New Zealand after a close contest throughout the season.

Commonwealth Games

2018 also saw good performances from the men's and women's sides at the Commonwealth Games in Australia, with both teams securing bronze medals. New Zealand won the two golds.

Rugby World Cup Sevens

England just failed to win the 2018 Rugby World Cup Sevens in San Francisco. Simon Amor's men relished the new 'winner takes all' format, beating Samoa, the USA and South Africa before falling 31-12 to New Zealand in the final. England's women were disappointed to lose to Ireland in the opening round, but rallied well and won the Challenge competition.

WOMEN'S SIX NATIONS

The 2018 Women's Six Nations was an important tournament for the Red Roses, coming soon after their narrow defeat to New Zealand in the 2017 Women's Rugby World Cup Final.

England, so often the tournament's champions, were edged out by a Grand Slam winning France. The decisive game came in the fourth round of matches, with English hearts being broken by a last minute try from Trémoulière. France won the game 18-17 and went on to clinch the title with a win over Wales.

England have won the tournament on 14 of the 23 times it has been played, with no less than 13 Grand Slams. With a record like that, they were never going to be satisfied with second place. However, there was some consolation

for head coach Simon Middleton, with comfortable victories over Italy, Wales, Scotland and Ireland.

Middleton fielded three players with over 100 caps during the campaign: captain Sarah Hunter, lock Tamara Taylor and prop Rochelle 'Rocky' Clark. Playing alongside these veterans were exciting young talents like Ellie Kildunne, Kelly Smith and Lagi Tuima. Only France, who England beat in the 2017 WRWC semi-final, could live with this blend of experience and fresh talent.

'Rocky' Clark who retired from international rugby at the end of July, 2018, remains England's most capped player (male or female), having racked up no less than 137 appearances by February 2018. Only Richie McCaw, Brian O'Driscoll and George Gregan can boast more caps than her!

ROUND 1

Venue: **Stadio Mirabello, Reggio Emilia**

Date: **4th February 2018**

Result: **Italy 7 / England 42**

Italy – Tries: Ruzza **Conversions:** Sillari

England – Tries: Bern, Hunter 3, Cleall, Dow, Kildunne **Conversions:** Daley-Mclean 2 **Pens:** Daley-Mclean

Three second-half tries from captain Sarah Hunter saw England stretch away from Italy after a hard-fought first half. A good start and a bonus point win for the 2017 Grand Slam winners.

ROUND 2

Venue: **Twickenham Stoop**

Date: **10th February 2018**

Result: **England 52 / Wales 0**

England – Tries: Cleall 2, Dow, Riley, Kildunne 2, Burford, Packer **Conversions:** Daley-Mclean 6

HRH Prince Harry was in attendance at the Stoop to see a commanding win over Wales. England were never in trouble and two tries apiece from Poppy Cleall and Ellie Kildunne meant the bonus point was a formality.

ROUND 3

Venue: **Scotstoun Stadium, Glasgow**

Date: **23rd February 2018**

Result: **Scotland 8 / England 43**

Scotland – Tries: Konkel **Pens:** Law

England – Tries: Waterman 2, Bern, Pearce 2, Kildunne, Tuima **Conversions:** Daley-Mclean 4

A seven-try haul, including doubles for Danielle Waterman and Charlotte Pearce,

meant England secured maximum possible points from the first three matches. 'Rocky' Clark became the game's fourth most-capped player.

ROUND 4

Venue: **Stade des Alpes, Grenoble**

Date: **10th March 2018**

Result: **France 18 / England 17**

France – Tries: Trémoulière 2, Drouin **Pens:** Trémoulière

England – Tries: Dow, Cokayne **Conversions:** Daley-Mclean 2 **Pens:** Daley-Mclean

France edged out England in the tournament decider. England showed great power throughout the match, but Jessy Trémoulière won the match with a last-minute try in front of 17,440 supporters.

ROUND 5

Venue: **Ricoh Arena, Coventry**

Date: **16th March 2018**

Result: **England 33 / Ireland 11**

England – Tries: Waterman, Packer, Cokayne, Kildunne, Reed **Conversions:** Daley-Mclean 4

Ireland – Tries: Molloy **Pens:** Tyrrell, Briggs

Danielle Waterman became England's leading try scorer with 47. The result was never really in doubt and England secured their fourth bonus point victory of the tournament.

KYLE
SINCKLER

Mr Impact!

An awesome presence in attack and defence. Sinckler is a prop who can run like a full back and tackle like the best, with three caps for the British and Irish Lions.

ENGLAND FACTS

10 things you didn't know about England Rugby …

1. England's first international rugby match was against Scotland in 1871. (England lost.)

2. England are the only northern hemisphere side to have won the Rugby World Cup.

3. England have played 723 international matches – won 397, lost 276, drawn 50.

4. England have been in the final on three occasions: 1991, 2003 and 2007. They won RWC 2003 in Australia.

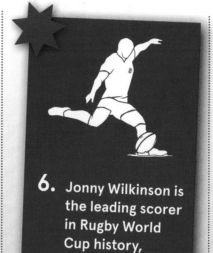

6. Jonny Wilkinson is the leading scorer in Rugby World Cup history, with 277 points.

7. England have had the most grand slam wins – with 13 for men and 6 for women.

8. Smith is the most popular surname for England Rugby players – with 14 internationals.

9. Rory Underwood has scored the most tries with 49 in total followed by Ben Cohen and Will Greenwood with 31 each.

10. England's largest attendance at Twickenham was March 2015 against Scotland playing in front of 82,319 fans.

England Rugby

5. Jason Leonard has played the most matches at Twickenham with 55. Dylan Hartley is catching up fast with 52.

Do you think Dylan Hartley can beat Jason Leonard's home match record?

England Great: Jonny!

Jonny's reputation was sealed in one unforgettable moment in November 2003, when he kicked a last minute, extra time drop goal to win the Rugby World Cup for England.

In 2003 England were undoubtedly the best team in the world, full of great players like Martin Johnson, Lawrence Dallaglio, Jason Robinson and Jonny himself. They progressed relatively easily to the final for a night of incredible drama which no-one in the stadium, or watching on television, could ever forget.

After a try from Jason Robinson and three penalties from Jonny, Australia's kicker, Elton Flatley, showed incredible nerve to land an 80th minute penalty - tying the game at 14-14 and leading the two exhausted teams into extra time.

Jonny and Flatley traded further penalties in extra time to leave the scores level at 17-17, with just one minute to play and the tie apparently heading to sudden death England mounted one final attack and, after several phases of play, Matt Dawson passed the ball to his fly half.

It is at moments like this that greatness is secured.

Jonny had to deal with unbelievable pressure. He had to overcome the exhaustion of playing 100 minutes of

JONNY WILKINSON IS THE MOST FAMOUS ENGLISH RUGBY PLAYER IN HISTORY.

Wilkinson was also the ultimate team player. Off the pitch he was humble and approachable, keen to help anyone he came across.

international rugby. He had to forget that he had already missed three drop goals that evening. He had to ignore the fact that he was forced to make the attempt with his weaker right foot, and that at least five desperate Australians were charging at him.

Somehow he overcame all these things and slotted the kick. England won the competition - and Jonny's legacy was assured.

Supremely talented, Wilkinson was also the ultimate team player. Off the pitch he was humble and approachable, keen to help anyone he came across. He became the ultimate rugby ambassador, showing everything that is great about the game.

A true legend!

27

HEADCASE

Playing rugby, like any sport, is a brilliant way to keep yourself mentally and physically fit. Taking regular exercise keeps you strong and healthy. Rugby is a great way to do this whilst making new friends and having great fun at the same time!

As with any sport, however, rugby can lead to injury. It's especially important to be careful with any impact or shock to the head – which can cause concussion.

To avoid injury make sure you know how to tackle properly, and respect rules which are there to protect other players – such as not tackling players whilst they are in the air.

You may see elite players being managed individually and temporarily go off pitch for a Head Injury Assessment. For everyone else, the RFU has clear guidance to look after you and get you back on your feet.

What is a concussion?

A concussion is a temporary injury to the brain that cannot be seen on routine x-rays or scans. It affects the way a person may think and remember things for a short time, and can cause a variety of symptoms.

The '4 Rs'

RECOGNISE

the signs and symptoms of concussion

REMOVE

the player from play

RECOVER

fully before returning to sport

RETURN

only after a graduated return to sport

SEARCH ONLINE...

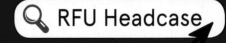
RFU Headcase

DID YOU KNOW..?

Why not amaze your friends with these incredible rugby facts and figures – who'd have believed it!

BEAT THAT!

England's highest-ever score was 134-0 against Romania in 2001.

RUGBY MILLIONS

More people play rugby in England than anywhere else in the world - over 2 million of them!

BORE-DRAW

0-0 draws were quite common in rugby's early days. The last time England were involved in one was against Ireland in 1963.

WHERE IT ALL BEGAN

Rugby began at Rugby School in Warwickshire in the 19th century. The boys invented their own game and it went around the world.[1]

50 NOT OUT!

England Sevens captain Tom Mitchell racked up his 50th HSBC World Rugby Sevens Series appearance at Twickenham in 2018.

BALL-TASTIC

The first rugby balls were made from pigs' bladders. These days things are a bit cleaner - and more controlled. World Rugby states that (for adults) a ball must be 28-30 cm long, made from 4 panels with a central diameter of 58-62cm and a pressure of 0.67-0.70 kg per square cm.

MURDERBALL

Australia are the current Olympic Wheelchair Rugby champions. When the game was first invented it was called murderball.

TRUE RUGBY LEGENDS!

The RWC 2019 mascot is called *Ren-G* and is based on mythical Japanese creatures called shishi. There is a parent and a child version of *Ren-G* and they represent rugby's international values: Integrity, Passion, Solidarity, Discipline, and Respect.

TOP RANKING

There are over 100 countries listed in the official World Rugby men's rankings. In June 2018 poor old American Samoa were the team with the most potential for improvement. They were ranked 105th and last. Come on the Talavalu!

SCHOOL BOY LESSONS

Several international sporting traditions began at Rugby School and were copied around the world. These include the tradition of awarding *caps* to recognise selection for a team and England wearing white jerseys.

---

[1] William Webb-Ellis was a pupil at the school, but didn't actually invent the game. If you want the full story why not visit the all-new World Rugby Museum at Twickenham.

ENGLAND ⊹
SUMMER TOUR
SOUTH AFRICA 2018

England won the third test against South Africa in Cape Town, bringing to an end an unwelcome sequence of five consecutive defeats.

South Africa took the series 2-1 but England coach Eddie Jones refused to be downbeat. He pointed out that many key players were missing from the tour, due to injury and the need to rest. He is also firm in the belief that great teams need to endure a period of difficulty – to learn lessons, to build team spirit and to become stronger.

There were encouraging performances from several players such as Tom Curry and Jonny May. Curry proved he is a player of genuine international class and May was the player of

the tour - constantly asking questions of the Springboks and scoring in each test.

The first test in Johannesburg was a historic occasion. Siya Kolisi became the first black player to captain South Africa. For many years, under the Apartheid regime, South African rugby and society was strictly divided along racial lines. Black players were not allowed to play for the Springboks, and the team was banned from international competition as a result, only returning in 1992.

1st TEST

📍 **Johannesburg**
South Africa 42 / England 39

A thrilling match with ten tries. England got off to a blistering start but then tired and allowed South Africa to come back. A late English rally was not quite enough. What a game!

2nd TEST

📍 **Bloemfontein**
South Africa 23 / England 12

Another strong start, with England 12-0 up after 12 minutes. However, they failed to score during the rest of the game as the Springbok pack got on top and clocked up the points.

3rd TEST

📍 **Cape Town**
South Africa 10 / England 25

At last! England prevail in wet conditions thanks to great teamwork, accurate kicking from Farrell and a touch of genius from Cipriani. A good end to a difficult season.

THE
GAME
OF OUR
LIVES

What does Rugby Mean to You?

🔍 #thisisrugby

We all agree that rugby is the greatest sport of all, but everyone has a different reason for loving the game.

Here are some people's contributions to the RFU's **Game Of Our Lives** campaign, with different people explaining 'What Rugby Means to You'.

Why not get an adult's permission and check out **#thisisrugby**?

> "IF IT WASN'T FOR RUGBY I'D STILL BE ON MY OWN... IT'S THAT OPPORTUNITY TO MAKE NEW FRIENDS AND TO BE PART OF SOMETHING, PART OF A TEAM
>
> I'M PART OF A TEAM AND THAT IS ITS OWN REWARD, I'D SAY COME ALONG AND GIVE IT A GO"

Alex, Hartlepool Rovers

> "WE WERE JUST LIKE FAMILY. WE LOOKED OUT FOR EACH OTHER. WE CARED FOR EACH OTHER."

Katy Daley-McLean

RUGBY IS BASED ON RESPECT AND INTEGRITY. NO MATTER HOW HARD A MATCH IS, I FIND SOMETHING THAT PUTS A SMILE ON MY FACE

John Goldman, Mill Hill RFC

RUGBY'S A SOCIAL GAME. I'VE STILL GOT FRIENDS THAT I USED TO PLAY WITH AT SCHOOL AND AT LOWER CLUB LEVEL

Courtney Lawes

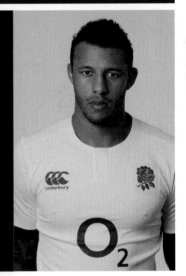

#THIS IS RUGBY

England Rugby

England Rugby

ELLIE KILDUNNE

Ellie Kildunne is the 18 year old who lit up the 2018 Women's Six Nations with a stunning individual try against Wales.

Receiving the ball just inside her own half, Ellie set off on an extraordinary run which saw her beat six players before touching down. It was a thrilling demonstration of pace, agility and spatial awareness.

Remembering the try Ellie said:

"I didn't expect Nolli (Danielle Waterman) to give me the ball as I was thinking I will just cover the back field, then all of a sudden it was in my hand.

"I read little cues and if I see a tiny gap, I always think I might as well see if I can try and get through it."

It was Ellie's second try of the match, and sealed a comfortable 52-0 win over the Welsh. England would go on to finish second in the table, just being edged out by France in their decisive fourth round fixture.

Ellie has come a long way in a short time. Growing up in West Yorkshire she started playing rugby league for clubs including Castleford. Her potential was obvious, and she managed to persuade her parents that it would be a good idea to move to Gloucester to pursue a career as an elite union player.

Rugby was not allowed to get in the way of studies, however. Throughout the 2018 Six Nations campaign Ellie was diligently

studying for her A-Levels in Biology, PE and Geography - occasionally calling on the expertise of the coaching staff for help with PE assignments!

Recently retired Danielle Waterman has become a mentor and friend to Ellie. The two have much in common. Both can play full back or elsewhere in the back line. Additionally, while now England's record try scorer, and a world cup winner, Danielle was once the youngest-ever player to represent England.

With a mentor like 'Nolli' and the rest of the England team at her side, there is no limit to what Ellie can achieve in the brave new world of women's rugby.

> "I didn't expect Nolli (Danielle Waterman) to give me the ball as I was thinking I will just cover the back field, then all of a sudden it was in my hand."

GUESS WHO..?

Can you guess who the players are in the portraits below?

ANSWERS ON PAGE 60

TOM CURRY

A dynamic flanker

...like his identical twin brother Ben, Tom was only 18 years old when he made his full England debut against Argentina in 2017.

LIFE IN THE ENGLAND CAMP

Have you ever wondered what it's like to be a professional rugby player?

TACTICS

EXERCISE

NUTRITION

SUNDAY

PLAYERS' ARRIVAL

Arrive at Pennyhill Park (The England team's training base in Surrey) in time for lunch. Some players will have media commitments, whilst others will be able to relax and have any minor injuries or knocks attended to. The players will eat together and begin to focus on the opposition and on tactics for the game.

TALK TACTICS

MONDAY

All members of the England senior squad will be in camp, mixing team training sessions with activities dedicated to their particular position or role in the team (front row, leaders, backs...).

TUESDAY

TRAINING SESSIONS

WEDNESDAY

Training includes some weights sessions, and plenty of time to rest and take on board food and drink to build up strength and energy.

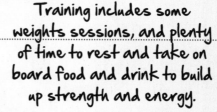

BUILD STRENGTH AND ENERGY

Playing rugby for England and your club is a full time job. Players need to train and look after themselves in the best way possible, to make sure they are ready for 80 plus minutes of intense physical effort. Here we take a look at some of the things that go on during a week before a Saturday away game during the Six Nations.

THURSDAY — TEAM ANNOUNCEMENT

The tension ratchets up a notch as the team announcement is made by the coach, with some players also made available to the media. Training sessions become less physical and players concentrate on their individual plays, tactics and approach to the game. Rest and nutrition are vital.

REST

FRIDAY

FINAL PREP

Some of the support staff will already have travelled to the match venue to prepare for the players' arrival. The team will have a morning training session, lunch and then travel to their hotel near the away ground.

SATURDAY — MATCH DAY! GO FOR IT!

Morning free for individual preparation as nerves begin to mount. The team have lunch together about three hours before kick-off, and arrive at the ground 90 minutes before the start.

Pre-match nutrition, strapping and preparation for the game before the anthems and kick off. After the game the coach and some players will give interviews.

All players and staff attend a formal dinner hosted by England for the away team before late night travel back to Pennyhill Park

DINNER

SUNDAY — POST-MATCH

The team spend the morning together, with post-match massages and any medical attention necessary. The players go back home after lunch, ready to return and start the preparation for the next match.

DIARY

TRAINING

CONTACTS

CHRIS ROBSHAW

One of the best tacklers in the world

A natural leader, Robshaw has led England on more than 40 occasions – including a historic 38–21 victory over New Zealand in 2012.

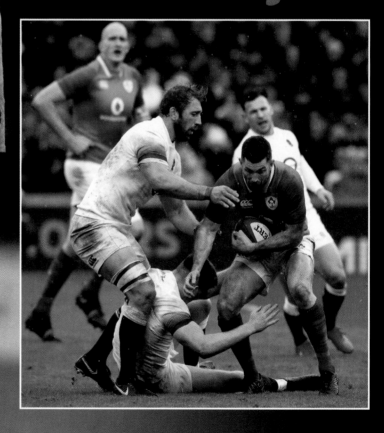

RUGBY WORLD CUP WORDSEARCH

Help Ruckley find 24 words relating to the Rugby World Cup. Look carefully - they might be vertical, diagonal or even back-to-front! Happy hunting! ANSWERS ON PAGE 61

G	T	M	K	N	O	I	T	A	C	I	F	I	L	A	U	Q	A	N
Y	N	L	C	D	T	G	K	P	F	M	R	A	D	H	C	N	F	D
A	I	G	R	O	E	G	G	N	L	Z	N	O	L	Z	I	H	D	N
K	R	K	N	V	C	X	H	E	K	I	Z	Z	M	T	E	G	V	A
R	M	I	H	G	F	Y	Z	W	F	T	M	M	N	A	C	Y	B	L
H	R	V	J	G	C	A	J	Z	K	L	Z	E	F	L	N	X	Y	E
Q	H	L	L	I	N	U	P	E	P	V	G	Z	H	B	A	I	N	R
J	X	D	G	V	F	G	O	A	Z	R	L	T	K	S	R	Z	A	I
T	G	H	W	X	M	U	O	L	A	X	B	F	O	M	F	R	A	G
H	O	P	F	Y	T	R	L	A	D	W	L	U	B	B	B	X	N	U	B
X	G	N	V	N	W	U	D	N	M	N	T	Q	B	L	W	X	S	F
N	Q	Z	G	G	M	N	R	D	Z	H	A	R	M	K	N	K	T	Q
M	Q	J	R	A	A	X	M	X	A	R	V	L	O	T	X	X	R	W
R	V	G	N	L	T	D	R	F	V	B	C	N	G	P	R	C	A	N
B	J	Z	T	O	K	Z	R	Y	J	A	P	A	N	N	H	L	L	L
N	M	O	K	N	P	I	J	V	U	S	A	B	L	M	E	Y	I	L
Z	C	Y	W	T	C	L	Y	L	A	T	I	D	Z	S	T	K	A	P
S	O	N	L	A	P	U	C	D	L	R	O	W	Y	B	G	U	R	K
T	C	M	X	M	B	O	N	U	S	P	O	I	N	T	W	H	T	N

- ☐ Ireland
- ☐ Scotland
- ☐ Japan
- ☐ Romania
- ☐ New Zealand
- ☐ South Africa
- ☐ Italy
- ☐ England
- ☐ France
- ☐ Argentina
- ☐ USA
- ☐ Tonga
- ☐ Australia
- ☐ Wales
- ☐ Georgia
- ☐ Fiji
- ☐ Uruguay
- ☐ Final
- ☐ Bonus Point
- ☐ Trophy
- ☐ Pool
- ☐ Tokyo
- ☐ Rugby World Cup
- ☐ Qualification

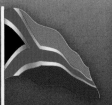

DANIELLE
WATERMAN

England Great!

England's highest-ever try scorer – 47 tries in 82 tests!

England
Rugby

SPOT THE BALL

Can you help Ruckley spot which is the real rugby ball in the picture below?

ANSWERS ON PAGE 61

GEORGE FORD

George Ford is a massively talented fly-half. Established by Eddie Jones as the country's first-choice No. 10, George's attacking skills and silky passing have led England to great success.

George is the son of rugby league legend, and successful union coach, Mike Ford. His ability in both codes was apparent from a very early age. He played league at a junior level for both Wigan Warriors and Bradford Bulls before switching to the 15 man code and joining Leicester Tigers' academy.

Amazingly, George was only 16 when he made his full debut for the Tigers. He became the youngest ever player in a professional union game when he faced Yorkshire Carnegie in 2009. Also making his debut in that game was George's brother, Joe - who was playing fly-half for the Leeds team! The brothers exchanged penalties throughout the match, but Joe and Leeds had the last laugh as they won 28-17.

This was one of very few reverses for George, who developed into a first-class rugby player at an incredibly young age. Never the biggest of players, his natural talent and sense of authority meant that he represented England at Under-16, -18 and -20 level - often being the youngest player in the team. After kicking

England to an U20 Grand Slam George was named IRB (World Rugby) Junior Player of the Year in 2011.

George's full England debut came in 2014, when he replaced Owen Farrell against Wales. The two players' careers have always been intertwined. Owen's father, Andy, was another rugby league great who later turned to union and coaching. The two boys were childhood friends (they both attended St George's School in Harpenden) and have kept up a strong friendship.

George knows that he will have to continue playing to the very highest level if he is to keep the No. 10 shirt. If he does so, he has every chance of being the man to mastermind an English World Cup triumph.

George became the youngest ever player in a professional union game when he faced Yorkshire Carnegie in 2009.

2018 MATCH STATS

Included here are the key stats from England's Six Nations games and the tour to South Africa.

SIX NATIONS

v ITALY

Venue: Stadio Olimpico
Date: 4th February 2018
Result: Italy 15 / England 46

ITALY
Tries: Bellini, Benvenuti
Conversions: Allan
Penalty: Allan

ENGLAND
Tries: Farrell, Ford, Nowell, Simmonds (2), Watson (2)
Conversions: Farrell (4)
Penalty: Farrell

v WALES

Venue: Twickenham Stadium
Date: 10th February 2018
Result: England 12 / Wales 6

ENGLAND
Tries: May (2)
Conversions: Farrell

WALES
Penalty: Anscombe, Patchell

v SCOTLAND

Venue: BT Murrayfield
Date: 24th February 2018
Result: Scotland 25 / England 13

SCOTLAND
Tries: Jones (2), Maitland
Conversions: Laidlaw (2)
Penalty: Laidlaw, Russell

ENGLAND
Tries: Farrell
Conversions: Farrell
Penalty: Farrell (2)

v FRANCE

Venue: Stade de France
Date: 10th March 2018
Result: France 22 / England 16

FRANCE
Tries: (penalty)
Conversions: (penalty)
Penalty: Machenaud (4), Beauxis

ENGLAND
Tries: May
Conversions: Farrell
Penalty: Farrell (2), Daly

v IRELAND

Venue: Twickenham Stadium
Date: 17th March 2018
Result: England 15 / Ireland 24

ENGLAND
Tries: Daly (2), May

IRELAND
Tries: Ringrose, Stander, Stockdale
Conversions: Sexton (2), Carbery
Penalty: Murray

....

QUILTER CUP

v BARBARIANS

Venue: Twickenham Stadium
Date: 27th May 2018
Result: England 45 / Barbarians 63

ENGLAND
Tries: Daly, Francis (2), Merer,
Launchberry, May
Conversions: Ford (6)
Penalty: Ford

BARBARIANS
Tries: Tries: Ashton (3), Vito (2), Russell,
Radradra, Timani, Laidlaw
Conversions: Russell (7), Laidlaw,
Fernandez Lobbe

SUMMER TOUR

v SOUTH AFRICA

Venue: Ellis Park Stadium
Date: 9th June 2018
Result: S.Africa 42 / England 39

SOUTH AFRICA
Tries: de Klerk, Nkosi (2), le Roux, Dyantyi
Conversions: Pollard (4)
Penalty: Pollard (3)

ENGLAND
Tries: Brown, Daly, Farrell, Itoje, May
Conversions: Farrell (4)
Penalty: Daly, Farrell

....

Venue: Toyota Stadium
Date: 16th June 2018
Result: S.Africa 23 / England 12

SOUTH AFRICA
Tries: Vermeulen, (penalty)
Conversions: Pollard, (penalty)
Penalty: Pollard (3)

ENGLAND
Tries: Brown, May
Conversions: Farrell

....

Venue: Newlands Stadium
Date: 23rd June 2018
Result: S.Africa 10 / England 25

SOUTH AFRICA
Tries: Kriel
Conversions: Jantjies
Penalty: Jantjies

ENGLAND
Tries: May
Conversions: Farrell
Penalty: Farrell (6)

England Rugby

XXI COMMONWEALTH GAMES RUGBY SEVENS

HSBC LONDON SEVENS

CROSSWORD

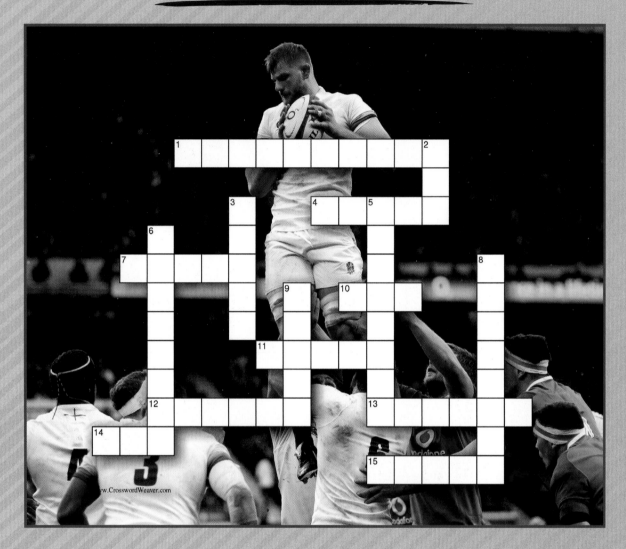

www.CrosswordWeaver.com

ACROSS

1 HQ, Home of England Rugby.
4 Hot on the pitch - played for England at only 18, Tom _ _ _ _ _.
7 Host of RWC 2019.
10 Worth 5 points.
11 You don't want to hit these.
12 Rugby Animals (1): Stripy beasts in the Leicester jungle.
13 The city where England won the Rugby World Cup in 2003.
14 Head Injury Assessment: abbreviation.
15 Rugby Animals (3): Argentinian national side.

DOWN

2 Jonny might play on the wing.
3 England's record points scorer _ _ _ _ _ Wilkinson.
5 Nickname for England Women's team.
6 Contested every year between England and Scotland _ _ _ _ _ _ _ _ Cup.
8 Numbers 6 and 7 on the rugby pitch.
9 Rugby Animals (2): the pride of Britain and Ireland.

ANSWERS ON PAGE 60

England Rugby

PLAYER PROFILES

MIKE BROWN

Club	**Harlequins**
Position	**Full Back**
Height	**1.83m**
Weight	**92kg**
Debut	**South Africa, 2007**
Caps	**72**
Points	**65**

DANNY CIPRIANI

Club	**Gloucester Rugby**
Position	**Fly Half**
Height	**1.85m**
Weight	**91kg**
Debut	**Wales, 2008**
Caps	**16**
Points	**64**

LUKE COWAN-DICKIE

Club	**Exeter Chiefs**
Position	**Hooker**
Height	**1.84m**
Weight	**112kg**
Debut	**France, 2015**
Caps	**7**
Points	**0**

Players and statistics correct as of June 2018. England caps and points only.

TOM CURRY

Club	**Sale Sharks**
Position	**Flanker**
Height	**1.86m**
Weight	**99kg**
Debut	**Argentina, 2017**
Caps	**4**
Points	**0**

ELLIOT DALY

Club	**Wasps**
Position	**Centre**
Height	**1.84m**
Weight	**94kg**
Debut	**Ireland, 2016**
Caps	**21**
Points	**57**

BEN EARL

Club	**Saracens**
Position	**No. 8**
Height	**1.82m**
Weight	**102kg**
Debut	**-**
Caps	**-**
Points	**-**

NATHAN EARLE

Club	**Harlequins**
Position	**Winger**
Height	**1.85m**
Weight	**99kg**
Debut	**-**
Caps	**-**
Points	**-**

OWEN FARRELL

Club	**Saracens**
Position	**Fly Half**
Height	**1.88m**
Weight	**92kg**
Debut	**Scotland, 2012**
Caps	**61**
Points	**690**

Players and statistics correct as of June 2018. England caps and points only.

GEORGE FORD

Club	Leicester Tigers
Position	Fly Half
Height	1.78m
Weight	84kg
Debut	Wales, 2014
Caps	47
Points	220

PIERS FRANCIS

Club	Northampton Saints
Position	Fly Half
Height	1.82m
Weight	92kg
Debut	Argentina, 2017
Caps	4
Points	5

ELLIS GENGE

Club	Leicester Tigers
Position	Prop
Height	1.87m
Weight	113kg
Debut	Wales, 2016
Caps	5
Points	0

JAMIE GEORGE

Club	Saracens
Position	Hooker
Height	1.83m
Weight	109kg
Debut	France, 2015
Caps	28
Points	5

JONNY HILL

Club	Exeter Chiefs
Position	Lock
Height	2.01m
Weight	112kg
Debut	-
Caps	-
Points	

NATHAN HUGHES

Club	Wasps
Position	No. 8
Height	1.96m
Weight	115kg
Debut	South Africa, 2016
Caps	17
Points	5

NICK ISIEKWE

Club	**Saracens**
Position	**Lock**
Height	**1.99m**
Weight	**113kg**
Debut	**Argentina, 2017**
Caps	**3**
Points	**0**

MARO ITOJE

Club	**Saracens**
Position	**Lock**
Height	**1.95m**
Weight	**115kg**
Debut	**Italy, 2016**
Caps	**22**
Points	**5**

JOE LAUNCHBURY

Club	**Wasps**
Position	**Lock**
Height	**1.96m**
Weight	**118kg**
Debut	**Fiji, 2012**
Caps	**54**
Points	**20**

ALEX LOZOWSKI

Club	**Saracens**
Position	**Fly Half**
Height	**1.84m**
Weight	**92kg**
Debut	**Argentina, 2017**
Caps	**4**
Points	**5**

JOE MARLER

Club	**Harlequins**
Position	**Prop**
Height	**1.84m**
Weight	**110kg**
Debut	**South Africa, 2012**
Caps	**59**
Points	**0**

JONNY MAY

Club	**Leicester Tigers**
Position	**Winger**
Height	**1.88m**
Weight	**90kg**
Debut	**Argentina, 2013**
Caps	**37**
Points	**85**

CHRIS ROBSHAW

Club	**Harlequins**
Position	**Flanker**
Height	**1.88m**
Weight	**109kg**
Debut	**Argentina, 2009**
Caps	**66**
Points	**10**

DAN ROBSON

Club	**Wasps**
Position	**Scrum Half**
Height	**1.70m**
Weight	**77kg**
Debut	**-**
Caps	**-**
Points	**-**

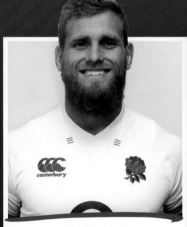

BRAD SHIELDS

Club	**Wasps**
Position	**Flanker**
Height	**1.93m**
Weight	**112kg**
Debut	**South Africa, 2018**
Caps	**2**
Points	**-**

SAM SIMMONDS

Club	**Exeter Chiefs**
Position	**Flanker**
Height	**1.83m**
Weight	**93kg**
Debut	**Argentina, 2017**
Caps	**7**
Points	**10**

Players and statistics correct as of June 2018. England caps and points only.

KYLE SINCKLER

Club	Harlequins
Position	Prop
Height	1.83m
Weight	113kg
Debut	South Africa, 2016
Caps	13
Points	0

JACK SINGLETON

Club	Worcester Warriors
Position	Hooker
Height	1.80m
Weight	108kg
Debut	-
Caps	-
Points	-

HENRY SLADE

Club	Exeter Chiefs
Position	Fly Half
Height	1.88m
Weight	87kg
Debut	France, 2015
Caps	13
Points	10

DENNY SOLOMONA

Club	Sale Sharks
Position	Winger
Height	1.80m
Weight	99.5kg
Debut	Argentina, 2017
Caps	5
Points	5

Players and statistics correct as of June 2018. England caps and points only.

57

BEN SPENCER

Club	**Saracens**
Position	**Scrum Half**
Height	**1.78m**
Weight	**83kg**
Debut	**South Africa, 2018**
Caps	**2**
Points	**0**

MAKO VUNIPOLA

Club	**Saracens**
Position	**Prop**
Height	**1.80m**
Weight	**121kg**
Debut	**Fiji, 2012**
Caps	**51**
Points	**5**

BILLY VUNIPOLA

Club	**Saracens**
Position	**No. 8**
Height	**1.88m**
Weight	**126kg**
Debut	**Argentina, 2013**
Caps	**36**
Points	**30**

HARRY WILLIAMS

Club	**Exeter Chiefs**
Position	**Prop**
Height	**1.90m**
Weight	**131kg**
Debut	**Argentina, 2017**
Caps	**11**
Points	**0**

MARK WILSON

Club	Newcastle Falcons
Position	Flanker
Height	1.88m
Weight	107kg
Debut	Argentina, 2017
Caps	4
Points	0

JASON WOODWARD

Club	Gloucester Rugby
Position	Full Back
Height	1.88m
Weight	100kg
Debut	-
Caps	-
Points	-

BEN YOUNGS

Club	Leicester Tigers
Position	Scrum Half
Height	1.78m
Weight	92kg
Debut	Scotland, 2010
Caps	77
Points	60

Players and statistics correct as of June 2018. England caps and points only.

QUIZ

PAGE 12-13

1) England v Wales
2) 2003
3) True
4) San Francisco
5) 134 – 0
6) Italy
7) Calcutta Cup
8) True
9) 15
10) 1987
11) Rochelle 'Rocky' Clark
12) Ireland
13) 82,500
14) Ren-G
15) 3

CROSSWORD

PAGE 50

```
T W I C K E N H A M
                A
    J         C U R R Y
    O         E      Y
C   N         D
J A P A N   L   T R Y   F
A   N     I       O     L
L   Y     POSTS   S     A
C         O       E     N
U         N             K
T I G E R S       SYDNEY E
H I A                    R
          PUMAS
```

GUESS WHO..?

PAGE 36

Jamie George

Courtney Lawes

Joe Marler

Rochelle 'Rocky' Clark

WORLD CUP WORDSEARCH

PAGE 41

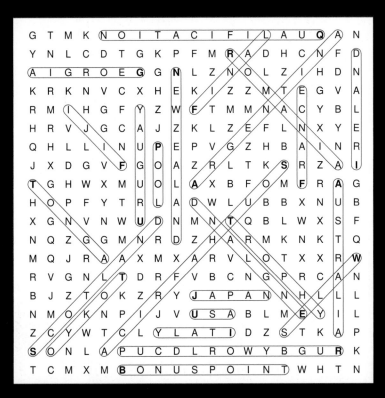

SPOT THE BALL

PAGE 43

WHERE'S RUCKLEY?

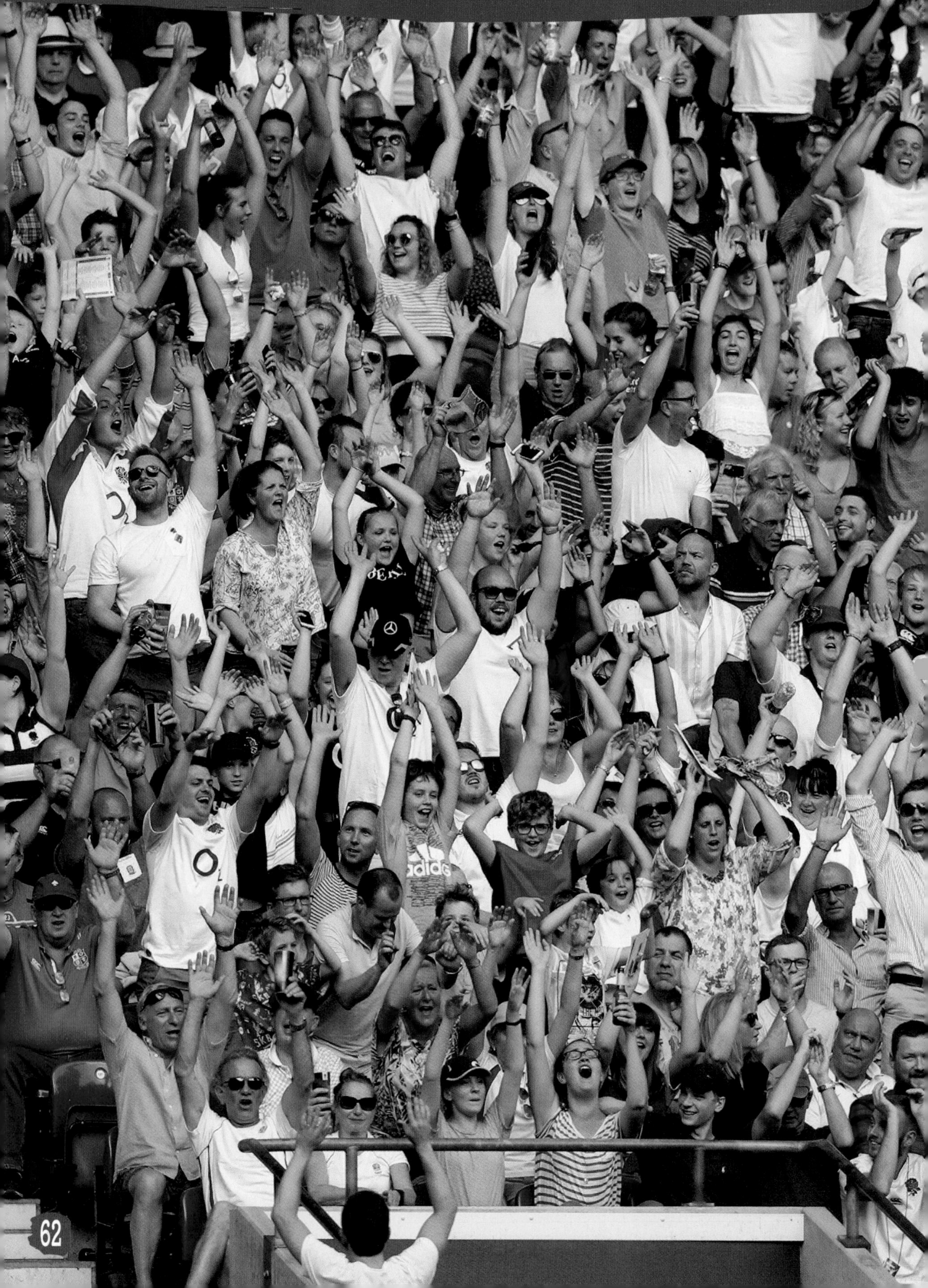